Dorothy May Mercer

<u>Two For One</u>
<u>Formatting Bargain Bundle</u>

I0484150

How To Design & Better Format Your Paragraphs
How to For You Series #7

Fix Paragraph Formatting in Word

Includes Bonus Book:
How to Format Your Book *For*
Publishing
How to For You Series #11

1

INTRODUCTION

Hi, Everyone,

In order to keep the prices as affordable as possible, the first How to For You series was published entirely in ebook format. Each book dealt with one issue, explaining it simply, step by step.

Since then I have been asked to publish them in convenient paper form. Authors need to have the book open on their desk, available for quick reference, as they follow the steps, one by one.

And so, to keep the cost down, I have combined the books in convenient bundles of two or three books each, in a logical group.

This "Formatting Bundle" starts out by teaching you how to format paragraphs in Microsoft Word and moves on to formatting your entire book. Makes sense, right?

So, let's get started.

How To Design & Better Format Your Paragraphs

Chapter One

Let's suppose your Ebook is finished, maybe even published. Oops! You notice that some paragraphs are block print, whereas some are indented, and some are spaced crazily. Some are justified, others aligned left or right. Some are different fonts. (Worse yet, some picky reviewer has remarked that "This would be a good book, if it were edited." Ouch!) You can go through the book one paragraph at a time or you can save yourself a lot of trouble, by using some commands available to you in Microsoft Word Version 2007 (and higher). We will discuss these instructions using Word 2007, but you can find similar commands in later versions of Word.

First-Make a Copy

Open up your book document in Word 2007 or later version. Make a copy, just in case you mess up. Work with the copy and save it under a new name. *If you know how to make a copy, skip the rest of this paragraph.*

Pull down the File menu and click "Save As". In the new window, enter a new name that is similar to the original, and click Save. I usually name this one the same name plus Copy 1. Now you will notice that the name will have changed in the far top of your document. At this point you are working with the copy, and you original is safely tucked away.

Remember it is important to Save your work from time to time.

Reverse and Forward Arrows

Click "Home". Notice the topmost icons, on the left. You should see two curlicue arrows. Hover your mouse over the arrows. One will say "undo typing (Control + Z)." Another will say "repeat typing (Control + Y)." These are very useful when you need to reverse a boo-boo, or restore something you accidentally erased. If you click on the arrow pointing left, it will reverse your most recent command. If you keep on clicking you will continue to reverse your recent commands, one at a time when you have made several mistakes in a row. Likewise, if you click on the arrow pointing right, it will restore your most recent command.

The Home Toolbar

Directly under these arrows is "Home." Click Home one time to open the Home toolbar. You will find most everything you need for this exercise on the Home toolbar. Notice the toolbar is divided into five sections, Clipboard, Font, Paragraph, Styles and Editing. We will be using the Paragraph and Editing, occasionally.

Tabs Are No-Nos

Let us suppose you have used "enter" and "tab" to start and indent the first lines of your new paragraphs. Unfortunately, sometimes you forgot the "tab" and sometimes you hit "enter" by mistake. The result was an irregular formatting of paragraphs. Not good. In fact, the Kindle instruction booklet specifically advises you not to use tabs at all. Kindle formatting cannot handle tabs. So, the first thing you must do is eliminate all tabs. Imagine trying to do this one at a time. Horrors!

Find and Replace

Fortunately, Word has already thought of this problem and designed handy-dandy little tools called "Find" and "Replace." You will find them in the Editing section of your Home toolbar.

First, we will find all the tabs in your document and replace them with nothing, thereby eliminating (deleting) them.

Move to the beginning of your document. To delete unwanted tabs, first open up "Replace". Enter a tab in the "Find what" space. Do not enter anything in the "Replace" space. Click "Find next." Nothing happens, right? In fact, the "Find next" command is darkened, indicating you really didn't type something in the "Find what" space. Okay, this is where you need to know the little trick I discovered. (Drum roll here.)

You cannot simply hit tab, you must <u>copy and paste</u> a tab command.

*It is possible to do this in your book document but just to be safe...*Save and keep your book document, and then quickly open up a new blank document. We will make some tab signs, just so we can copy one. Make sure your Show/Hide feature is on "Show." Hit tab a few times. Notice the little arrow appears and your cursor jumps forward. Highlight and Copy one arrow (tab command). This saves it in your clipboard folder. You won't see it, but, trust me, it's there.

(Now you can close the fresh document. No need to save it.)

Move back to your book document. Open "Replace" again. Place cursor in the "Find what" space and click Control plus the letter V. This will paste one tab in that space. You will not actually see a tab arrow, but you will notice your cursor will have jumped ahead the space of one tab. That will confirm that the tab command is really in there. Now the "Find next" command will be available to you. Do not enter anything in the "Replace" spot.

Click "Find next" and your cursor will jump ahead and highlight the first tab it can find in your book document. If you hit "Replace," your program will erase that tab. You will notice that your document will show that the tab was replaced with nothing, thus it was erased.

(Remember your handy "Undo typing" command, in case of an error.)

If all is well, you can click "Find Next," and then "Replace all." This will get rid of all the tabs in your entire document.

Format Paragraphs

Highlight—Select—All

Now you are probably ready to format your paragraphs. Under the Editing section of your Home toolbar, click Select and then Select All. This will highlight your entire book. *(See exception, later.)*

Home Toolbar—Paragraph Section

Indents and Spacing

Next click the tiny arrow at the bottom right of the Paragraph section of the Home toolbar. You should be in the "Indents and Spacing" tab. Here you can decide how to format all your paragraphs. You may choose to indent the first line so many spaces, 1, 2, 3, etc. If you prefer blocked paragraphs, you may choose to set the paragraphs so many lines apart.

Kindle suggests you do one or the other, not both. In other words, do not indent the first line and place blank line spaces in between paragraphs, as well. That is, if you indent the first line, set the paragraph spacing at zero. The default may show auto, or 6. Be aware you can erase that and type in a zero or whatever you wish.

Line and Page Breaks

Under the "Line and Page Breaks" tab, it is good to check "Widow/Orphan Control". This prevents your book from leaving half sentences dangling all by themselves— another thing that annoys picky editors. I prefer "Justified" paragraphs, for a more professional look in printed form especially, but you may choose "Left Alignment." One way or the other it is important to be consistent.

Line Spacing
You may also choose to space the lines, single space, double space, or something in between. I like to set my line spacing at "Multiple, 1.15" to give just a tiny bit of extra white space between lines. Personally, I do not like double spacing for books. Select what you choose, or type in a number by hand. (Note: In this document the lines are spaced 1.15 apart, the paragraphs are justified and set .6 before. You like?)

Select "Whole Document" and Click OK at the bottom of this window and your entire document will be changed. All your paragraphs will look alike. Save your document. Return to Home. Scroll through your book to check it.

Now, anytime you hit "enter" just once, a new paragraph will be started in the format that you have specified. No more need for tabs; no need to hit enter twice. Next time your write a book, save yourself some trouble and set it up this way before your start.

Exception

(Exception: There may be an occasion when you wish to change the formatting in just one paragraph or one section. In this case, after you have formatted the entire book correctly, merely highlight the section or paragraph you wish to format differently. Next, use all the commands under the "Paragraph" menu, as above. Click Ok and the changes will only affect the part that you highlighted.)

Now, you are all set and you have learned some new skills... unless...

Too Many Enters

All right, maybe you are not quite finished fixing things. Let's suppose that your document is loaded with "enters". Maybe you went crazy with entering "enter". Oops! Kindle recommends no more than three enters in a row. Why not? Because it is very annoying to the person reading your ebook. Enter requires them to scroll down, maybe even going so far as move to the next page.

This tires them, and overworks their poor finger. Tsk-tsk.

Page Break

It is better to use "page break" than to place a line of "enters" to format your pages. You will find "page break" under the "Insert" tab. It is good to enter no more than three "enters" followed by a page break after your title page, table of contents and at the end of each chapter.

Also, Kindle recommends you space your chapter endings exactly the same, for a uniform appearance. At the end of each chapter, I place two enters, a page break, the new chapter heading or title and one more enter, before I start the first paragraph of each new chapter. This leaves a uniform amount of white space around all my chapter headings.

Perhaps, you may have hit "enter" twice after some paragraphs and not others. Remember you have already formatted the space between paragraphs, using the Paragraph menu. Now, you only need one "enter" at the end of a paragraph. There is nothing else to do but get rid of those extra "enters." The extra "enter" problem is difficult to fix, globally, in Word 2007, but it can be done, (drum roll here) as follows:

Instructions for 2007 only. Scroll down for instructions for later versions.

1. Navigate to the beginning of your document (or to the beginning of the place you wish to edit).
2. Toggle the paragraph sign to "on" so that all the signs show in your document.
3. Go to your "Insert" menu and click "Symbol" (on the far right).
4. Pull down the menu and search under "More symbols" until you find this symbol: ^
5. Highlight and Insert the ^. Copy and erase the ^ *(highlight and click Ctrl + X).* Now you should have the ^ erased and hidden on your clipboard.
6. Next, open the Find/Replace window.
7. Place your cursor in "Find what" and paste the ^ (Ctrl + V).
8. Type p, leaving no spaces. Now you should have ^p in the "Find what" space.

9. Do not type anything in the "Replace with" space.

10. Click "Find next". The next "enter" sign (paragraph character sign) in your document will be highlighted. You may have to scroll up or down to see it if it is hidden behind the open "Find" window.

11. Decide whether you want to delete it, or leave it as is. If you wish to delete it, click "Replace". The program should delete the sign, replacing it with nothing.

12. Click "Find next". The program should jump to the next "enter" sign. Continue until the end.

13. Under File, click Save.

Note: (Sometimes you cannot spot the darned highlighted "enter" symbol. Not to worry. You can always close the "Find" window and look for the symbol. When you reopen the "Find" window the commands should still be there. Simply proceed to find the next. When you get to the very end of your document, the program may ask you whether you want to continue or start again at the beginning. It is a good idea to do that, just to double check, in case you missed one.)

Instructions for Word 2010 and later:

1. If you are lucky enough to own Word 2010 or later, this is how to fix double "enters".
2. Go to the beginning of your document.
3. Select the Home tab.
4. Go over to the far right and click "Replace". A new window opens.
5. Place cursor in "Find what".
6. Pull down the "Special" menu (near the bottom) and click the first item on the list,"Paragraph Mark" (not Paragraph character).
7. An entry will appear in the "Find what" that looks like this: ^p.
8. Leave the "Replace with" area blank.
9. Now click "Find next".
10. Your first "enter" paragraph character will be highlighted.
11. Decide whether to keep it or delete it. To delete it click "Replace".
12. To keep it, do nothing. Instead, proceed to the next paragraph character by clicking "Find Next". Again, decide whether to delete it or keep this one.
13. Proceed through your entire document in this fashion until you

have removed all of the unwanted characters.

14. Under File, click Save.
15. Return to Home.

Now is a good time to turn off the show/hide control and scroll your entire document. I like to change the view to one page for this step. Is it formatted correctly?

Congratulations. You are ready to finish preparing your book for Kindle. Need help with that? See my article, "How to Prepare Your Book for Kindle," available on Amazon in ebook format.

Happy publishing.

If you appreciate my efforts, kindly post a nice review on Amazon.com. Better yet, like and buy my books. That would be ever so nice of you.

Thanks a bushel and a peck, and a hug around the neck.

Comments? Questions? Go to MercerPublications.com and Select Guest Book. Or check out our facebook page-- The Savage Surrogate, or see us on Twitter at DorothyMMercer.

Thank you for purchasing, "How to Design and Better Format Your Paragraphs". We hope you enjoyed and found at least one helpful tip. Please encourage other writers by posting a short, positive review on the Amazon or other site where you purchased this book. Go to one of the following Amazon pages:

Amazon USA www.amazon.com

Amazon United Kingdom www.amazon.co.uk

Amazon Canada www.amazon.ca

Amazon Brazil www.amazon.br

Amazon Mexico www.amazon.com.mx

Amazon France www.amazon.fr

Amazon Italy www.amazon.com.it

Amazon Denmark www.amazon.de

Amazon India www.amazon.in

Amazon Australia www.amazon.com.au

And while you are there please consider another book or booklet by this author.

Suggestion: Place some of my books on your "Want to Buy" list. Easy-Peezy and free.

Links to all of these books can be found at www.mercerpublications.com

Now that you have all your paragraphs in perfect form, please continue on for How to Format Your Book For Publishing.

How to Format Your Book for Publishing

How to For You Series #7

TABLE OF CONTENTS

Introduction

When I write a book for publishing, I decide whether this will be a print book, an Ebook, or both. Why is this necessary? Because the formatting is different.

This article will explain how to format your book, adapt it for print and for Ebook, and explain the similarities and differences. You will begin with a "plain Jane" format and adapt that to the different versions.

As is the case with all of the "How To For You" series, the instructions are for Microsoft Word 2007, or higher. However, a computer savvy person may be able to adapt them to other word processing software.

Chapter 1 Designing Pages and Type

Paragraphs

It is always best to format your paragraphs before you begin typing. Go to the Home toolbar and pull down "Paragraph." Everything you need is here. Decide how to space and indent your paragraphs and lines. You can always change it later. For detailed instructions and recommendations please see my Ebook, "*How to Design and Format Your Paragraphs.*"

Page Layout

Use the "Page Layout" command to design your pages, margins, orientation, and size. It is best to choose from among the "standard" sizes. The most popular sizes for novels, in inches, are 5x8, 5.25x8, 5.5x8.5 and 6x9. More industry-standard sizes are 5.06x7.81, 6.14x9.21, 6.69x9.61, 7x10, 7.44x9.69, 7x9.25, 8x10, and 8.5x11. When choosing a size, things to consider are whether this is an adult or children's book, an illustrated book, or a series. Consider how many pages you expect to have. A rule of thumb might be this: a longer novel requires a larger size, and vice versa. It is all right to set your book size and margins now, before you begin. This will not affect your later Ebook versions.

Margins

For a print book, use the "custom" margins command. Under "multiple pages" click the "mirrored" margins command. Set all the margins to .5 (point five). Set the gutter to .3 unless it is an unusually thick book (over 100,000 words) in which case you might choose .4. This will determine how close to the spine your words begin. Everyone hates to have words disappearing into the center of the book. However, bear in mind that each increase adds more pages, thus more cost, to your book. Even the tiny change of .1 on your paragraph indents will increase/decrease the total pages.

Line Spacing

Unless your book is a novella, short story, or booklet (approximately under 30,000 words) I recommend setting the sentence spacing at 1.15. This will add just enough white space between the lines for ease of reading, without adding a lot of pages. Aim for a balance of white space on your pages, to avoid an appearance of overcrowding. Also be aware that, although the program offers a few default sizes from which to choose (such as 1, 1.5 and 2) it is easy to simply type in the size you want. The same is true of paragraph spacing and indentation. You can easily type over the default sizes.

Formatting Bargain Bundle-Two For One

In the case of a smaller book, you may want to set the line spacing to 1.5 or 2, thus increasing the number of pages. However, at this point, you may have no idea how long your book will be. In this case, set the line spacing at 1.15 or 1.2. When the entire book is written you can change it. More on that later.

Typeface

On the Home toolbar, choose a typeface and type size for the body of your book. A good way to do this is to type a sample paragraph, highlight it and scroll through the available typefaces to see which one shows best. Copy and paste this same paragraph three or four times. Highlight the second paragraph and choose a different typeface and size for this. Do the same with the third, fourth and so on. Print out this sample page. Compare and choose the best one for your print book. Most printers can duplicate all but the weirdest typefaces. You are aiming for the best possible clarity in print, while maintaining a style in keeping with your book. For instance, an historical novel will not use a very modern looking print. I happen to like Microsoft sans serif in size 12, but that is my preference for a contemporary paper book, because it prints clearly. For an historical novel I would probably stick with Times New Roman, in size 10 or 12. (We old-timers can remember when that was the only choice.)

Any Ebook conversion will use its own typeface, anyway, so, in that case, it does not matter.

Once you have made your choice, select the Home toolbar again. Highlight the paragraph of your choice. Right click on "Normal." Left click on "Update Normal to Match Selection." In the future, you will use this Normal to write most of the body of your book. There may be occasions when you need to set off a small section. In that case you can reset the style by hand, or choose among the other styles. More on that later.

Chapter 2 Style Your Chapter Headings.

Type a sample heading and copy it three or four times. Highlight the first sample and scroll through Heading 1, Heading 2 and Heading 3 on the Home toolbar. Keep going for as long as you wish. (This is fun, right?)

Move over to the "Styles" section and pull down the menu. Move your mouse up and down through these selections to see what happens and your type quickly changes from one to the other. You may decide to use the default setting for Heading1, but, if you see something you like better, click on it. Otherwise, go to the Home toolbar and select from the fonts available. Try bold, underline and italic. Once you make a choice, you may change Heading 1 to reflect that choice, using the same technique that you used to select Normal. (That is, select your sample, right click Heading 1, left click Update Heading 1 to Match Selection.) It is very important to use the same Heading 1 for all your chapter headings, not only for the sake of consistency, but for later, when and if you install an interactive Table of Contents such as the Table of Contents you see at the beginning of this book. (For more info, please see my Ebook, *"How to Install an Interactive Table of Contents.)"*

If you decide to use sub-headings, you will use Heading 2 in the same fashion. Examine the Table of Contents in this book, again. Notice that I used Headings one, two and three. Neat, eh? For your convenience I placed a bookmark in the Table of Contents, so that you can travel there with one click. A click or Ctrl + click will bring you back here to Chapter 3. (Note: These two commands only work if you are reading an Ebook.)

Chapter 3 Order of Opening Pages

You will begin your opening pages in a preordained order.

Title page (always on the first odd numbered page*)

ISBN, Copyright notice, publisher, permission and rights statement. (These items can go on one or two pages, as desired.)

Optional endorsements, reviews and ads.

Optional acknowledgements

Optional dedications

Table of Contents

Introduction or Prologue, if any (odd numbered page*)

Chapter One (odd numbered page*)

Always end each opening page with a page break, not a series of enters.

*Note: In the case of a print book, placing certain important pages on odd number pages will insure that they appear on the right hand page.

Note: Your print book's opening pages should be spaced and centered so that the text is nicely balanced on the page. I usually go to View/Two Pages, so that I can look through the opening pages side by side. This will help me to space the text nicely. Use the enter command to space your text down from the top of the page, and your alignment commands (left, center, right, justified) to position text. You may also use your space bar to move text to the right.

Remember: Do not use tab to position text, as it is not allowed in the Kindle Ebooks.

Hint: Depending on whether you selected to indent the first line of your paragraphs, the enter command may not place your text entirely flush with the left margin. If so your Center command will not precisely center. You can overcome this by positioning your cursor in the offending space and clicking Backspace once, before you click the Center command.

Hint: If your Enter command is not giving you the exact amount of space you desire, change the font size in that particular white space. This will change the height of your Enter.

The Reverse Arrows

Now is a good time to mention a very useful tool, the reverse or undo and redo commands. Locate the curlicue arrows in the upper left of your display. These little arrows can be useful to you in many instances, for example when you wish to reverse a previous keystroke. Each time you click on a curlicue arrow it will reverse one previous stoke or command, in the direction of the arrow.

Common Mistakes:

When designing your opening pages, always end the page with a page break, or one or two enters followed by a page break rather than using a long line of "enters" to start a new page. This is true for Ebooks, as well as print books. Later we will change the size and spacing a bit for your Ebook. For now, space your opening pages as if it is a print book.

Do not use "tabs" to position your titles. Instead use the Home/Paragraph/Center command, or the left, right, justified commands. Be aware that Kindle does not allow "tabs."

Chapter 4 Pictures

Certain books are meant to be picture books. If so that is an entirely different kettle of fish, requiring a book of its own. (coming soon, *How to Design a Picture Book*). However, you, the author, may desire to entire a picture into your story by way of illustration, such as a drawing or map etc. This requires a special set of tools.

First of all, be very careful when entering pictures in color. You can use them without an extra charge in an Ebook, but color print is very costly. For print, it is best to keep your interior in black, white and gray scale, while your cover is in color. More on how to do that, later.

First, click you cursor in the place where you wish to insert a picture. Go to the Insert menu and choose the type of item you wish to insert. For now, choose Picture. A new window will open up allowing you to scroll through everything stored on your computer. Click your choice. Its title will appear at the bottom of your display. Click Insert and your choice will jump into your text.

We will not go into the use of copyrighted pictures, here. The subject is long and murky. When in doubt, a web search will provide more info. Just be careful that any picture you use is one that you own, have licensed, or is in the public domain. When posting pictures of people, in many cases you should have permission, unless it is a crowd shot in a public place. For example I paid a license fee to use this picture of models.

Now, you can resize the picture and format it in several different ways. Move to the center of the picture and a four-headed arrow will appear. Click here and notice that a new choice appears in your toolbar, entitled Picture Tools/Format. Click Format and a marvelous new toolbar appears with all kinds of goodies that you can use to change your picture. One of the first things you might do is to open Size and locate the Lock Aspect Ratio Relative to original picture commands. Make sure these are checked. This will prevent you from turning the figures into skinny or fat people. Now you can resize the picture while keeping the same aspect. The easiest way to change the size is to click the picture once, and then move your cursor around the edges of the picture. Double arrows will appear. Left click and hold one of the corner arrows. Drag it in and out until you find the size picture that you want.

Next, experiment with the various commands on the Picture Tools/Format bar, until you gain an understanding of what is available.

Hint: Be aware that Ebooks have a special way of handling pictures, so until you understand that, you may want to avoid pictures altogether.

Hint: You may use color in Ebooks. But, a print book will charge a lot more for colored interiors, of any kind, whether it is a full color picture, or a mere footnote with one little letter in color. Here is what you do:

When formatting your color picture for a print book, open the Picture Tools/Format by clicking once in the center of your picture. Click Format. In the far left of this toolbar, in the Adjust Section, click Color. Your picture will appear in a variety of colors. Choose one of the black white and gray tone samples. Now your picture will print nicely without extra charge.

Moving Your Picture

You may easily move the picture around by a maneuver called drag and drop. That is, holding a left click in the center of the picture, move your cursor to a new location and release the mouse button. You can also move it by grabbing the tiny anchor that (sometimes) appears next to the picture, drag and dropping it to the new location.

So far, your picture has taken a space between lines of text. However you can arrange your text to flow around the picture, as seen above.

Click once in the picture. Notice that grab handles appear around the edges, indicating that the picture is selected. Open the Picture Tools/Format toolbar. Go to the Arrange Section and pull down the Wrap Text menu, using the tiny arrow under the words Wrap Text. Select the way you wish to wrap your text. A good choice is Tight. Now, move your picture and text to take the most advantage of the text wrapping. You want it all to make sense, that is, don't chop words in two. Besides moving the picture, you can easily arrange the particular text, by using your space bar or your enter button. You can also highlight the text involved and justify it right, left, or center. After you are satisfied with the result, please save.

Hint: A word of caution, speaking from experience. Do not get too carried away by entering multiple pictures, shapes, and/or clip art. After all, your goal is to write a book, not a photo album, which requires a whole new set of skills.

Chapter 5 Writing Your Book

Designing Chapters

Now, at last, you are ready to begin writing your book. Always start the Prologue and/or first chapter on a right hand (odd numbered) page. It may be necessary to insert a blank page to make this work. (Note: For your Ebook, this rule does not apply.) Sometimes authors will start all of their new chapters on the right hand side (odd numbered page) even though it may require entering a blank page. This is nice, but not required. Whatever way you do it, be consistent.

Hint: Any blank pages that you enter will have to be removed later when you design your Ebook version.

Always end your chapters with a Page Break. This is true for print and Ebooks alike. You may decide to place one or two enters before your break, or before your chapter heading. However you decide to do this, remember to do it the same each time. Click the Heading command. The word Chapter and the number will often enter automatically. You can change this or add a title to it, if you choose. Click enter and the program should switch to Normal and will go to the beginning of the first paragraph. Verify that you are in Normal, now.

Styling Non Fiction

Generally, if your book is non-fiction it will proceed by chapters and sub-chapters, in much the same fashion as this book. You may even use sub-sub chapters. Notice on the Home/Styles menu there is provision for Headings 1, 2, 3 and 4. Also, there is a variety of handy styles that you can use, such as "Subtle Emphasis," "Emphasis," .and "Intense Emphasis" Take a few seconds to check them out. You may use the suggestions given or create your own, as explained above.

A good way to understand this is to type a small throw-away sample, select it, and then scroll through the various options to see what happens to your sample. Unless you have a huge computer display, probably all the samples will not show. Try pulling down the menu using the arrows. You will be amazed at all that is available to you. For even more fun, pull down the Home/Change

Styles menu and scroll through the dozen or so dizzying array of styles. Should you run out of ideas there is even a provision to create your own style set. Try not to spend all morning playing around with this. Remember, you are going to write a book.

Styling Fiction

Generally a chapter in your fiction book will consist of a progression of scenes. If these scenes repeat in the same location on the same day there is no problem for the reader. But, if there is a change of location, a different set of characters, and/or a skip in time, the author must use a simple device to indicate the change. After all, one cannot start a new chapter for every simple change. Not only might the result be annoying to the reader, it could result in hundreds of chapters. And so, some simple device must be chosen. I have seen lots of different choices, some quite fancy, and I admire, even envy, that. But, for myself, I prefer to make it easy, lest I waste time fooling around with doodads. Sometimes all that is needed is space. If your paragraphs are not separated by lots of space, already, simply click in one or more extra ~~carriage returns~~, (oops) enters. (Darn! I dated myself, again.)

The reader will catch on quickly that extra space means a change of scene.

On another occasion, thinking I was smart and creative, I chose a fancy gizmo to mark my change of scene. After I uploaded my book to Kindle publishing, I used the review window to check the result. $%#$@^! The Kindle converter had changed all my pretty gizmos to placeholders. They would not convert. Back to the drawing board to change every single one of those fancy gizmos to something more generic.

Sometimes I use a character on my computer keyboard. Examples:

***

^^^^

^^*

~~~~~

Once you make a choice, stick with it for the remainder of that book.

I even went so far, once, to actually center the gizmo, as below. However, I soon discovered that was too much work, also I forgot half the time and had to go back and fix it, and so I simply moved my gizmo to the left and continued in that fashion for the remainder of the book. My readers do not seem to mind. It is best not to annoy the reader with too much fal-de-rall.

***

Hint: Sometimes when you type in a string of characters the Word program mistakenly thinks you want it to go all the way across the page, like this:
■■■■■■■■■■■■■■■■■■■■■■■■■■■■■■■■■■■■■

You can fix that by clicking Backspace just once, and then retyping your characters. Be sure and do this right away, before you go on because, later on in your novel, it is impossible to go back and delete the thing. If there is a way, I haven't found it.

Alignment

Compare the following two paragraphs, not as to content, but in terms of how they look, at first glance.

#1.When setting your paragraph style, you have a choice of left, center, right and justified. Personally, I like to use justified in my novels. It makes for a much neater looking page. When a potential customer browses through a bookstore display, what attracts them? Is it the cover, title, author?

Perhaps it is all the above. Watch it happen, sometime. You will see the customer pick up the book, look at the cover, peruse the back cover, and finally flip through the pages. At this point, what is she looking for? My guess is that he is checking to see what the pages look like. Are they easy to read? Are they crowded or neat? Is the type clear and bright? If so, having the print justified will make it look neat and tidy.

#2. When setting your paragraph style, you have a choice of left, center, right and justified. Personally, I like to use justified in my novels. It makes for a much neater looking page. When a potential customer browses through a bookstore display, what attracts them? Is it the cover, title, author? Perhaps it is all the above. Watch it happen, sometime. You will see the customer pick up the book, look at the cover, peruse the back cover, and finally flip through the pages. At this point, what is she looking for? My guess is that he is checking to see what the pages look like. Are they easy to read? Are they crowded or neat? Is the type clear and bright? If so, having the print justified will make it look neat and tidy.

Paragraph #1 above, was left aligned, with no space between the paragraph and the preceding paragraph. The line spacing was set at "single."

Paragraph #2 was justified, with a space between paragraphs set at 10, and line spacing set at 1.15. See the difference? I think you will agree that paragraph # 2 appeared to be easier to read, even though it contained the exact same words, font and size as paragraph #1. The white space made the difference.

Chapter 6 After "The End"

Non Fiction

Footnotes
Footnotes are frequently used in non-fiction, but rarely, if ever, used in books of fiction. They serve the purpose of further explanation of a word or phrase, when the author does not wish to put it in the text. Another purpose is to identify and give credit to the origin of a quote, phrase or idea. This works well if the footnote is reasonably short, but in the case of long items, it is better to use an end note. Your software will give you the choice of footnote or endnote. It will place a tiny half-raised number exactly where you place your cursor, and open up an

area at the bottom of the page (or at the end of the book, as the case may be) where you type your note. In a well-constructed book, the reader can click on the number and be taken directly to the note. After reading the note, he can click back to the exact spot where he left off.

Hint: You will find the footnote and endnote commands in the References toolbar, Footnotes section. More advance commands are available in the pulldown menu, accessed by clicking the tiny arrow in the bottom right corner of the section.

Hint: When your book is converted to Ebook, the server (such as Kindle) will automatically place all your footnotes at the end of each chapter.

Reference Pages

Depending on the degree of formality of your book, following the end, it is quite proper to add any or all of the following references:

End Notes

Credits

Bibliography

Author's Notes

About the Author (with or without picture and address links.)

Note: If you are writing a formal college theme, thesis or dissertation, or a professional paper, there are strict guidelines for exactly how these references are to be written. We do not intend go into that, except to advise you, if that is your purpose, to please look for a more complete reference.

Fiction:

Typically, authors and publishers take advantage of the end space to lay in a bit of advertising. There are no strict rules for this, but it can range among these items:

A plea for Reviews

About the Author

Picture of Author

Author's Notes

Other books by this Author with titles, synopsis and/or where to order.

Cover Pictures of other books by this author, and/or this publisher.

Teaser peeks and chapters of the next book in the series, or others.

Almost anything goes, so long as it is lawful.

In my McBride Series, of five complex and full-length novels, I include a list of characters at the end of each book. Perhaps this is a bit unusual, but it helps the reader because there are a lot of characters in these books. I even use the reference myself.

Chapter 7 Final Formatting of Print Book

Assuming your book is completed, edited and proofread, multiple times, and you have saved a Plain Jane version, you are now ready to prepare it for printing. Send any previous versions to your Trash Can.

Save two more versions and label them Print Version and Ebook version. Open the print version. Check your opening pages one more time to ascertain that they are properly centered on the page. Click Save.

Creating Sections

In order to complete the following instructions please ascertain that the "show paragraph enter sign" is toggled on. I cannot draw one here, but it looks like a P backwards. When the sign is "on" you will see one of those backwards P's every time you push the enter key. The sign is located on the "Home" toolbar.

Move to the very end of your opening pages (just before your first chapter or intro.) and position your cursor just ahead of the "page break." Delete this "page break," temporarily.

Leaving cursor in place, open "Page Layout."

Click the tiny arrow next to "Breaks" and pull down the menu.

Under "Section Breaks" select "Next Page, (Insert a section break and start the new section on the next page)." This will re-enter the page break and add a section break as well. You have now divided your book into two sections for the purpose of entering different page numbers and headings in the second section.

Remember how you created two sections, because the time may come, after you have finished your book when you may wish to create a third section at the end, affording yourself the ability to have different headers in your advertising pages, especially if they contain a sneak peek of a few chapter of your next book. Don't worry about that now. Just remember where you found these instructions.

Creating Headers

Move your cursor into the first page of section 2 and click in the empty heading space, at the very top of the page.

Hopefully, the heading space will open up and the main body will be darkened. Everything you write here will show on every page in section two. In a moment we will write in this space. But first, if a header space did not open up, we need to find the Header and Footer Toolbar, as follows:

Click "View" and make sure you are in the "Print Layout" view. If not, click on it.

Now move back to "Insert" and click on it. Look for a section marked Header & Footer. You should see three choices, Header,

Footer and Page number. We will be using these three, eventually. Click on "Header." A new list will open. Click on "Type text" and watch what happens. A new toolbar will open called "Header and Footer Tools/Design."

Click "Design"

In case you are lost, let me repeat this sequence for you in one place:
View
Print layout
View
One Page
Insert
Header
Type text
Design

In the Header & Footer Design Toolbar you should see a "Navigation" section and an "Option" section. Your cursor should now be located in the header section of your page. Notice that this place is identified as 'Odd Page Header Section 2' and "Same as Previous" We are going to get rid of the "Same as Previous" label notation, as follows:

In the Navigation section, click once on the words "Link to Previous." This should delete that link and the "Same as Previous" words will disappear. In a moment we will do the same thing for the even pages in section 2, but first...

In the Option section of the Header & Footer Design toolbar, confirm that you have a check mark in all three of the choices:

√ Different First Page

√ Different Odd Even Pages

√ Show Document Text

Good! Almost there!

Now click the down arrow twice to take you to the header of page two, which will show "Even Page Header, Section 2" and "Same as Previous." You will delete the "Same as Previous" words in the same way you did it for the odd pages, i.e. Click "Link to Previous" in the Header & Footer/Design toolbar in order to toggle that link to off position.

One more thing...while you are in this toolbar, notice the Position section, containing the settings "Header from Top" and "Footer from Bottom." Set each of these to 0.3 (zero point three). This will position your headers and footers within their respective section, .3

(three line spaces) away from the edge of
the page. If you do not do this your printer
may cut off your wording in these sections.
Remember when we set the margins at .5?
Good. Now all your headers and footers will
be alike.

Now, you are ready to design your headers.

Designing Your Headers

Place your cursor in the header space for
page two or any one of the even numbered
pages. Any even page will do. (Change one
and you change them all.)

In this header, type the heading for your
even pages. Remember, even pages will be
on the left when you open your book. On this
page you will put the name of your book, and
any other item you wish to add, such as a
sub-title. You can position this right, left,
center or justified using the justification
commands and the space bar. Do not use
tabs. Also, remember the tip about centering,
i.e. make sure your text is flush with the left
(using backspace if necessary) before you
hit center. While you are designing this text,
feel free to use font, size, bold, italic and
underline, as seems good to you. Some folks
even have a logo that they put here.

Remember this will show at the top of every even page, so keep it small and informative.

You will *NOT* put a header on page one of your book, as this is a place to be fancy, and do something different, if desired.

Next, move your cursor into the header of page three and design the odd page heading. This is the place to put the author's name. Again, design it as desired.

Now, reading across left to right, the reader will see your book's name followed by the author's name. Good. This will remain the same throughout all the pages of the second section of your book, unless, someday later, you create a third section.

Installing Page Numbers

Now you are ready to install page numbers. Your cursor should be anywhere in section two. These commands are found at Home/Insert in the Header & Footer section. Choose bottom of page and select from the options available on the pulldown menu. Later you may choose "Format Page Numbers" from the same menu. Open that command and select "Start at" and enter the number 1. You do not want it to "continue from previous section," because we are going to do something different in the previous section, which was section one, remember?

Earlier when you were designing the headers, you selected "different odd and even pages." Because of that you may need to go to an odd page and insert page numbers, the same as you did on the even page. Just make sure that you are in section 2 (not 1) and that you format the numbers the same way that you did on the even page.

SAVE.

Flip through a few pages to make certain that everything is correct, including your headers and page numbers.

Next you are ready to format headers and footers for section one, i.e. your beginning pages. It is customary to leave the headers blank, but it is your decision as to whether or not you wish to have page numbers in the footers of the beginning pages. Sometimes they are omitted. But, you can install them the same way you did in the main body of your work.

My practice is to install page numbers here, using Roman Numerals (i. ii, iii iv, etc.) But, it takes extra time, so use your judgment.

TIP: If you find something is already written in the headers and footers of the opening pages, it means that you have made a mistake. You must return to the instructions for turning off "Same As Previous" at the beginning of Section 2, and make sure the "Link to Previous" button is turned off at the beginning of that section. Then you can go back to the headers of Section One and erase (delete) them.

TIP: If that doesn't work, you probably made a mistake in the instruction as to setting Section Break markers, found in the "Final Formatting Your Print Book" chapter.

Sorry, but you will need to go back and repeat. Do not despair. Remember, practice makes perfect and this is a complex learning experience. Do not expect to do it correctly the first time. Believe me, I still goof up. But, it becomes easier each time.

Did you install a Table of Contents? If so, you will need to update your table and make sure it is correct. For detailed help see my How to For You booklet, *"How To Install an Interactive Table of Contents."*

Note: Savvy computer geeks will find everything you need under Home/ References/ Table of Contents/ Update Table.

SAVE.

Remove All Color

One last thing to check: You must make sure that the interior of your Print book has no color. First, check any pictures and make sure they are in gray scale. If not follow the previous instructions found in Chapter Four Pictures.

Next, go to Home/Select and click Select All. Return to Home/Font and open the Font Color menu. Select Black. Click anywhere in a margin to turn off Select All.

Save a PDF Version

Now, you are ready to SAVE AS a PDF. Go to "File," Click "Save As." At the bottom of the next window locate "Save as Type." Pull down that menu and select PDF. Make sure the title is the way you want it. Click Save.

Now you should have four versions of your book in your special folder, as follows"

- My Book. Plain Jane
- My Book. Ebook
- My Book. Print
- My Book Print PDF

Close all versions you have open and open your Ebook version. You are now ready to prepare your Ebook version.

Take a break.

Chapter 8 Format Your Ebook

Break's over. Wake up your computer and get set to work on the Ebook version. Now that you are a pro, this will be easy-peezy.

You now have a Plain Jane version that has been saved as Ebook. There should be no headings and no page numbers. However, color is perfectly all right. Color pictures, color fonts—no problem. Also, please leave in the page breaks that you inserted earlier, that is, one at the end of each beginning page, and one at the end of each chapter. This will not cause readers any problem, but will make certain that important things begin at the top of a page.

The only changes that are necessary are to remove excess blank lines and blank pages. Simply go in and remove them. A few blank lines are fine, but no more than two in a row. That is all. See? I keep my promises, *most times*.

SAVE

Ads and Links

Now, think about whether there is anything you would put in an Ebook that you would not have in a print book. For example, you may put links after the end. These could be links to sales pages, other books, blogs, web pages, and so on. More than likely your readers will be reading this in digital form and will be hooked up to the internet. Therefore, you can insert links to various sites where you will invite your readers to explore. If you are unsure how to do this, see my "How To For You" booklet, *"How to Install a Link in Your Document."*

SAVE

You now have an Ebook version which can be the basis for any Ebook you wish to publish, such as Kindle, Smashwords, Nook etc. Each one has its own special instructions for preparation. My "How To For You" series has a book of detailed instructions entitled, "*How To Prepare Your Book For Kindle.*"

At this time you may want to have a PDF version of your Ebook for your own use. Simply follow the previous instructions for creating a PDF, taking care to label this version properly.

We Appreciate Your Business!

Thank You !

Dear Reader.

Was this book helpful to you? Did it deliver as promised? If you liked this it, please do me favors:

- Please go to Amazon and leave a simple, but nice, five-star review.
- Thanks a million.

(Not many folks will take the trouble to post a review, and even fewer will bother to copy and paste it in other marketplaces. You are truly one in a million! Three Cheers!)

- If you purchased this book, I know you will not "return" it for a refund. Sometimes, customers do so, perhaps unaware that it puts a black mark on the author's record. Amazon keeps track of these things.
- If you used the Amazon library option, and borrowed this book, you may return it, now, and borrow it again, anytime. You may even buy it. Whee!

While you are there, please consider buying/borrowing another book by Dorothy May Mercer. Or, you may consider the Want-to-Buy option and put several books on your "Add to Wish List." Amazon notices everything! Besides, this list makes a good suggestion list for your next birthday or anniversary wish list.

Another good option is the "Give As a Gift." Amazon sends a beautiful gift card to the recipient. You can add your own special message. Easy-Peezy.

Two easy ways to find all of the Dorothy May Mercer books:

1. Go to www.MercerPublications.com for links.

   Tip: Look at the "How to For You" menu for 19 helpful books for authors and indie publishers.

2. Go to any Amazon site and search for Dorothy May Mercer.

   Tip: There are four Amazon pages for her books. The control at the bottom of the first page will navigate you to any page of her books.

Thank you for purchasing this "How to For You" Series. We hope you enjoyed and found at least one helpful tip. Please encourage other writers by posting a short, positive review on the Amazon or other site where you purchased this book. Go to any and all of the following Amazon pages:

Amazon USA www.amazon.com

Amazon United Kingdom
www.amazon.co.uk

Amazon Canada www.amazon.ca

Amazon Brazil www.amazon.br

Amazon Mexico www.amazon.com.mx

Amazon France www.amazon.fr

Amazon Italy www.amazon.com.it

Amazon Denmark www.amazon.de

Formatting Bargain Bundle-Two For One

Amazon India www.amazon.in

Amazon Australia www.amazon.com.au

And while you are there please consider another book or booklet by this author. Links to all of these books can be found at www.mercerpublications.com

The complete "How to For You" **series of booklets for improving writers.**

1. How to Write Sentences and Paragraphs *in Your Novel*
2. How to Install a Link in Your Document
3. How to Sell Your eBook Using Amazon Free Days
4. How to Prepare Your Book for Kindle
5. How to Fix Errors in Your Document, *Find and Replace Globally*
6. How to Use Your Book for Free Ads
7. How to Design and Format Your Paragraphs
8. How to Design a Kindle eBook Cover

9. How to Install Your Kindle Cover on Createspace, *and Vice Versa*
10. How to Add an Interactive Table of Contents
11. How to Format Your Book, for Publishing–*Two Editions, Ebook and Print*
12. How to Edit a Book, *With a Friend–Two Editions, Ebook and Print*
13. How to Write Great Dialog–*Two Editions, Ebook and Print*
14. How to Market Your Book, *Marketing 101–Two Editions, Ebook and Print*
15. Bargain Bundle, Two For One, Includes #8, 9-Print Edition Only
16. Bargain Bundle, Two For One, Includes #14, 6-Print Edition Only
17. Bargain Bundle, Three For One, Includes #14, 6, 3-Print Edition Only
18. Bargain Bundle, Two For One, Includes # 7, 11-Print Edition Only
19.

Coming soon: "Now That You're On Your Way, What Next?" "Marketing 201"

The McBride Series of Action Novels, Starring Det. Lt. Michael J. McBride Jr.

A Series for Those Looking for Good Clean Cop Stories

"Car oo6 Responding" (Proceeds to Police Charities)

"The Cocaine Chase"

"The Immigrant and the Golden Coin"

"The Cartel Wars"

"The Gang Bust"

The Washington McBride Novels, Starring Senator Mike McBride, his wife Juliette, featuring his bodyguard, Cynthia Patterson:

"the Fairfax Fix"

"the Arlington Alias"

"the Savage Surrogate"

The McBride Romances:

"Fran and Max" *The Bungalow*

Coming in 2015 "Cynthia and Dan"

Photo-Travel books by Dorothy May Mercer, author, and Dave Mercer, photographer:

"Alaska and Back" With Dave and Dorothy.

"Africa and Back" With Dave and Dorothy

"Hawaii and Back," Vol. 1 Kauai" With Dave and Dorothy

"Hawaii and Back," Vol 2, Maui, With Dave and Dorothy

"Hawaii and Back," Vol 3, Oahu, With Dave and Dorothy

Coming in 2015:

"Hawaii and Back," Vol 4, The Big Island, With Dave and Dorothy

"Arizona and Back," With Dave and Dorothy

More books by Dorothy May Mercer:

"Leon and Esther," an historical Christian love story.
"Stories I Haven't Told," an auto biography
Other Author's Books published by Mercer Publications & Ministries, Inc.:

"Stormy Affair," a Romance, by Netty Ejike
"Sensual Bond," 5 Part Saga Series, by Netty Ejike

"He Called Her Hat," That Tough Little Lady, Amusing Historical Biography, by Myron C. McDonald

"Notes From John," Messages from Beyond, by Marcia McMahon

"Remember How Much I Love You," Romantic Suspense, by Dale L. Williams, M.D.

"The Inheritance From Hell," True Drama, by R.D. Margot

"Ascension Teachings," With Archangel Michael, by Marcia McMahon

Thanks, Again.

See you soon, in another book.

Dorothy May Mercer, Author Extraordinaire

Have a wonderful day!

We would love to hear from you. The best way to show appreciation to an author is to leave a review.

I read them all, over and over and over. True! Oftentimes I leave you a comment, as well.

Thank you!

Have a great day, and happy
writing.

Your pal,

Dorothy May Mercer

For prices and ordering information please go here:

www.MercerPublications.com

www.Amazon.com/DorothyMayMercer

More Entertaining Books from Mercer Publications, Inc.

In business since 1993

by Dorothy May Mercer and other distinguished authors:

McBride novels available-- Ebook and Print formats.

Starring Det. Lt. Mike McBride

The McBride Series:
- "Car oo6 Responding"
- "The Cocaine Chase"
- "The Golden Coin"
- "The Cartel Wars"
- "The Gang Bust"

The Washington McBride Series

Starring Senator Mike McBride

- "The Fairfax Fix"

- "The Arlington Alias"
- "The Savage Surrogate
"Starring wife Juliette McBride, investigative reporter

and Lady Dog, famous Seal-trained tracking and service dog.

The New McBride Romances Series

Fran and Max, the Bungalow

GO HERE TO ORDER THIS AND PREVIEW OTHER EXCITING AND ENTERTAINING NOVELS:

- http://www.MercerPublications.com

Historical books by Dorothy May Mercer:

- "Leon and Esther," an historical Christian love story.
- "Stories I Haven't Told," an autobiography

Travel Books With Colored Photographs:

By Dorothy May Mercer and Photographer Dave Mercer

"Alaska and Back" With Dave and Dorothy, a travel journal.

"Africa and Back" With Dave and Dorothy, a travel journal with color photographs.

"Hawaii and Back" Vol. 1 Kauai, With Dave and Dorothy

"Hawaii and Back" Vol. 2 Maui, With Dave and Dorothy

"Hawaii and Back" Vol. 3 Oahu, With Dave and Dorothy

Coming soon: "Hawaii and Back" Vol. 4 The Big Island, With Dave and Dorothy

Books edited and published by Mercer Publications & Ministries, Inc.:

~Recommended~

- "He Called Her Hat," That Tough Little Lady,
  by Myron C. McDonald

- "Notes From John," by Marcia McMahon

- "Remember How Much I Love You,"
  by Dale L. Williams, M.D.

- "The Inheritance From Hell," by R.D. Margot

- "Stormy Affair" by Netty Ejike
- "Sensual Bond" 5 Part Romantic Saga